MW00633509

Our Puget Sound
Backyard Birds

One couple's collection of candid bird photographs

Craig Johnson
Joy Johnson

Limited Edition, 1000 copies

ORANGE SPOT PUBLISHING

PREFACE

Natives of Western Washington, Craig and Joy grew up sailing, camping and hiking around the beautiful Puget Sound with their families. This connection to nature has persisted for them as a couple and has become an integral part of their relationship, continually leading them to explore the outdoors.

While not advocates of caging birds, they acquired a bird as a nestling many years ago. Caring for this bird for more than a decade, regularly observing her behaviors and unique characteristics, increased their knowledge and appreciation of birds in general. Feeding wild birds in the backyard spurred their curiosity to find out more about each bird that came by, which led them to study ornithology and to go birding multiple times each week.

As a watercolor artist with a marine art business, Craig was accustomed to photographing vessels as research from which to paint. It was natural for him to begin photographing birds as they stopped by for a bite to eat and while out in the field. Using a modest 400mm, f/5.6 lens, rather than the more advanced equipment used by most bird photographers, all photos were taken without a tripod in the yard or while out hiking. These images aided Craig with his avian paintings and many were artistic works on their own. With enough photos compiled to create a book, Joy was then able to apply her research and writing skills to help make the book flow.

By self-publishing this book, their goal is to share the delight they have experienced in their birding adventures. As supporters of wildlife preservation organizations, they will commit proceeds from the sales of this book to continue these efforts.

Watercolors by Craig Johnson

ORCAS ISLAND

N
W · E
S

SKAGIT
VALLEY

Puget Sound
Washington

Location
Map

WHIDBEY

Using symbols

Featured locations are listed below in alphabetical order
next to colored bird symbols. Page numbers follow.

Match colored bird symbols to same on map to find area
where birds were spotted. Corresponding pages in book
also show matching colored bird symbols in lower,
outside corners.

EVERETT

ISLAND

KINGSTON

EDMONDS

SEATTLE

Purple Finch, male

Golden-crowned Sparrow, juvenile

Each morning, our backyard fills with the chatter of a multitude of birds calling to one another and busily consuming their first meal of the day. Providing a yard free of pesticides allows the birds to begin foraging for a meal of insects.

Soon we replenish the feeders with fresh black oil sunflower seed, millet seed and suet. Thistle seed and hummingbird nectar are added during the spring and summer. With clean water poured into the bird bath, the feeding area is ready. The pleasure of watching a variety of birds visit the yard throughout the day is our reward for this effort.

Brown-headed Cowbird, male

Black-capped Chickadee

Red-breasted Nuthatch, female

With its decurved beak, the Bewick's Wren is ideally suited for extracting insects from an old garden fence. We also see it frequenting our neighbor's squirrel feeder (above left), possibly searching for more arthropods or, perhaps, seeking temporary shelter.

This little bird produces a beautiful song, projecting it with great enthusiasm.

Ruby-crowned Kinglet

Black-headed Grosbeak, Male

Spotted Towhee

Poised and ready, birds eagerly await an opportunity to make a dash for their food of choice. The need to constantly feed keeps them busy all around the yard for much of the day.

Dark-eyed Junco

Steller's Jay

These birds' vibrant colors intermittently adorn our yard while they take turns at the various feeding stations.

House Finch, male

Evening Grosbeak, male

Band-tailed Pigeon

Steller's Jay

Pileated Woodpecker

Pine Siskin

Northern Flicker, male

We have often witnessed these
different species of birds sharing
the yard in close proximity with
surprisingly few disputes.

Anna's Hummingbird, female

Rufous Hummingbird, female

Rufous Hummingbird, male

Anna's Hummingbird, male

Hummingbirds are great fun to watch. Their aerial antics seem to defy gravity. We listen for their distinctive clicking/chirping noise while out on hikes and in our own yard. With a backyard feeder and a fresh supply of hummingbird food, it is possible to get a closer look at these amazing little birds.

Anna's Hummingbird, female

Varied Thrush, male

Bushtit, female

It is always interesting to look out and see which birds happen by on any given day.

The feisty Red-breasted Nuthatch flies in, takes one sunflower seed and is off to stash it in the bark of a nearby tree.

Red-breasted Nuthatch, male

This tiny, well camouflaged Brown Creeper sunbathed at the base of a Douglas fir tree in our yard. The bird stayed several minutes before resuming the never-ending task of insect gleaning.

One regular visitor to the yard is this American Crow. Even as other crows retreat, it will continue foraging when we go out to fill the feeders. Sometimes we will toss it a few peanuts, which it promptly shells and eats.

Last summer, the same crow brought its fledgling to the yard to feed. After that, we often saw the bird perched with its mate and young in a dogwood tree near the corner of the yard, allowing us to witness their fascinating social interactions.

Sparrows, Juncos and other small birds must be on guard at all times, never knowing when one of these cunning and lethal predators might suddenly appear.

Sharp-shinned Hawk, juvenile

Sharp-shinned Hawk, adult

Glaucous-winged Gull

While many birds can be seen in one's own yard, getting out to natural areas can provide a wealth of bird species that may never make it to the typical suburban neighborhood.

To view waterfowl and seabirds, we have found that the **Mukilteo-Clinton Ferry** is a great place to begin.

Harlequin Duck, male & female

Barrow's Goldeneye, females

Western Grebe

Caspian Tern

Great Blue Heron

Red-breasted Merganser, female

The ferry makes a great platform from which to see birds riding the waves, both near the shore and further out on the water. Binoculars can be very helpful for viewing them.

Red-breasted Merganser, male

Surf Scoter, male & female

Golden-crowned Sparrow

Brewer's Blackbird, male

Possession Beach, on the south end of Whidbey Island, is a quiet little park with woodland, marsh and shore in close proximity. This allows an array of birds to come into view even if you remain stationary.

Northern Flicker, male

American Goldfinch, female, winter

American Goldfinch, female

American Goldfinch, male

19

Springtime at Possession Beach
can be especially entertaining.
Listening to the birds singing
here on a sunny day is a great
mood elevator.

At this time of year, birds may be more visible as they tend to be focused on finding a mate and preparing their nest.

This Song Sparrow continued to sing as we walked quietly along a path directly below.

Black-headed Grosbeak, female

Langley, in Southeast Whidbey Island, has a charming small town feel. From the vantage points along Cascade Avenue to the public hiking trail system through the woods, birding opportunities are plentiful.

Downy Woodpecker, female

Townsend's Warbler

Driving near Langley at dusk, we spotted this Barred Owl in a tree not far off the road. Keeping a respectful distance, we were able to observe the owl for quite a while without disturbing it.

The Eagles Nest Inn, near downtown Langley, has a serene, wooded setting which allows an abundance of birds and other wildlife to coexist on its ample property. With feeding stations set up near the inn, guests can view a wide variety of birds at close range.

Rufous Hummingbird, female

California Quail

Ruby-crowned Kinglet

Walking around the grounds of the Inn or into the woods that connect to the extensive public trail system, there are even more birds to be found.

Northern Harrier, female

Northern Harrier, female

Crockett Lake, in Central Whidbey Island, is a marshy area where saltwater and freshwater meet. Home to many bird species, some year 'round and others just passing through on their migratory journeys, this area has provided us with a multitude of birding opportunities.

Tundra Swans

Red-tailed Hawk, immature

Savannah Sparrow

Northern Harrier, male

Muted brown and green foliage contrast with bright blue water to make a colorful tapestry over which the Northern Harrier glides with seemingly effortless grace. This impressive bird flies low over the marsh, ready to take a small animal by surprise.

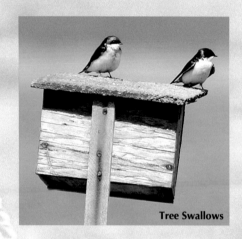

Tree Swallows

Great Blue Heron

Dunlin

Red-winged Blackbird, male

European Starlings

Driving by the lake along Highway 20, we look for birds perching on old fencing or posts, like this Western Meadowlark sunning itself.

At first glance, this area might seem rather barren, but when searching, there are many birds to be found.

Early winter brought a rare visitor to the area. As we were walking past the driftwood near the beach, a large white and gray bird flew up from the ground nearby. At first we thought it to be a gull, but quickly realized it was a Snowy Owl! When exiting the park just before sunset we discovered it again, this time perched on a log.

Short-eared Owl & Northern Harrier

One late winter day, we spotted this Short-eared Owl on an old pile in the grass. Later, it was exciting to watch it fend off a Northern Harrier who was interested in hunting for a twilight meal in the same territory.

On another visit, the owl to the left was stretching after pausing on what remains of an old sign.

Short-eared Owl

Perched atop a thorny branch, this Northern Shrike surveys the area. Although this songbird appears innocuous, the shrike demonstrates its true nature when prey is within striking distance.

Near the beach by Crockett Lake, a lone Killdeer
blends with the rocks among the bright spring foliage.

Great Blue Heron with chicks

Tall pilings at the **Keystone Ferry Terminal** provided an unlikely shelter for a Great Blue Heron to nest. The parent of these chicks was very diligent about standing guard.

Pigeon Guillemot, winter

Red-necked Grebe, winter

From the floating dock at Keystone State Park, we have watched birds dive underwater to pursue prey and then sometimes emerge very close to us.

Rhinoceros Auklet, spring

Rhinoceros Auklet, winter

Pigeon Guillemot

Belted Kingfisher, female

Keystone is clearly a popular place for birds to fish. Many aquatic birds come into the calm, protected harbor near the ferry terminal to catch a meal. It is interesting to compare the different fishing techniques employed by a variety of birds.

Belted Kingfisher, male

Great Blue Heron

Red-breasted Merganser, female

An unusual sight for this park was a lone Black Oystercatcher. This bird was content to go about its business of foraging and even napping while we sat on the beach nearby.

Long legs and bill help this sandpiper to be proficient at locating small fish and aquatic worms along the shore.

Greater Yellowlegs, juvenile

Pelagic & Double-crested Cormorants

Double-crested Cormorant, adult & juvenile

Common Loon, spring

Double-crested Cormorant

Common Goldeneye, male

With wings spread for maximum drying, this sturdily built cormorant shares the old pier with a host of other seabirds. Large webbed feet, powerful beak and long neck make this bird adept at hunting under water. Teal colored eyes gleam like gemstones from its dark, velvety looking feathers.

Goslings

Canada Geese, with their
V-shaped migrating flocks
and musical honking, are a
familiar sight around Puget
Sound. These large birds
primarily graze on wetland
or cropped field vegetation.
Sometimes a stray bird of
a different species will tag
along with the flock.

Canada Geese adults, goslings and domestic companion

Merlin, female

Mourning Dove

American Pipit

Savannah Sparrow

Birds can be found at both the shoreline of the Sound as well as inland areas by Crockett Lake. A banquet of insects exists among the driftwood here to accompany other foods available in nearby flora.

Song Sparrow, juvenile

Barn Swallow

Northern Shrike

41

Chestnut-backed Chickadee

The grounds at **Fort Casey State Park** have yielded numerous bird species during visits we have made there. It is always enjoyable to revisit familiar birds and exciting when we catch sight of a new one.

Yellow-rumped "Audubon's" Warbler, female

Red-breasted Sapsucker

42

A lone Mourning Dove perching high in a tree close to Admiralty Head Lighthouse kept a watchful eye on us as we admired it. The tall trees, dense foliage and open fields in this area offer abundant food sources for a great many birds.

Mourning Dove

Orange-crowned Warbler

Brown Creeper

Typically, smaller birds like these flit around so quickly that they are hard to see and especially difficult to photograph. This makes it even more delightful when they pause long enough for a portrait.

Golden-crowned Kinglet

Bewick's Wren

Spotted Towhee, male

Pileated Woodpecker, adult & juvenile

Entering the more densely forested areas of the park, numerous avian conversations can be heard before actually sighting any birds. As our eyes adjust to the shade, we look for specific birds we can hear near the ground, like the distinctive *to-wheee* of the Spotted Towhee or the curious *kip-kip* of the Winter Wren. Up higher in the trees, we might hear one of the woodpeckers either tapping or calling long before we see it.

Winter Wren

American Robin, male

Hairy Woodpecker, female

Bushtit, female

The American Robin's song sounds
very cheerful and inviting.

American Robin, male

Northern Rough-winged Swallow

Cedar Waxwing

Hermit Thrush

At times other birds add to the chorus in the park, drawing our attention to them.

Learning to recognize different species' songs can be helpful when identifying birds in the field.

House Sparrow, male

Olive-sided Flycatcher

Northern Flicker, male

We watched this male Northern Flicker preen on a fir branch for some time. When finished, he launched into flight, leaving behind a small tuft of down feather on the tree. Craig was pleased to have captured the burst of action and vibrant color of this handsome bird.

Merlin, female

Old fence posts along the farm roads to **Ebey's Landing** are sometimes occupied by birds of prey, like this Merlin resting with its left leg pulled up.

Lincoln's Sparrow

White-crowned Sparrow

At Ebey's Landing State Park, shrubs and brush give shelter and forage areas to many small birds. A hiking trail here takes us up high onto the bluff where we have observed larger birds flying by at nearly eye level while they ride the thermal wind currents.

The rocky shoreline at Ebey's Landing is one place we like to view water birds. Gulls and sandpipers will sometimes linger at the water's edge, allowing us to watch them at a comfortable distance.

Heermann's Gull

Black Turnstone

Glaucous-winged Gull, first winter

Grebes occasionally come close to the beach in search of prey. Some, like this Horned Grebe, display dramatic changes between muted winter and elaborate breeding season plumage.

Horned Grebe, winter

Horned Grebe, early spring

Horned Grebe

Flying low over the beach at **Coupeville**, this immature Bald Eagle was apparently challenging the territory of an adult eagle. Talons extended, the two met in flight with the adult quickly convincing the youth to move on.

Great Blue Heron

Coupeville has an active waterfront bird population. The Belted Kingfisher and Great Blue Heron hunt in the shallower water around the pier while Rock Pigeons and gulls rule the rooftops. Bald Eagles survey the scene from the sky and tall trees.

Belted Kingfisher, male

Bald Eagle, adult

Rock Pigeons

Red-tailed Hawk

Near **Joseph Whidbey State Park**, Northern Whidbey Island, we spotted a very large, stunning Red-tailed Hawk perched on a telephone pole, as they often do near farmland or pastures. We admired the bird from a distance and, after a while, watched it launch itself from the pole, letting out a loud screech as it ascended into the early evening sky.

Least Sandpiper

Killdeer

Common Snipe

Kah Tai Lagoon is a jewel of a park located in Port Townsend. The marshy, saltwater/freshwater combination here attracts a multitude of bird species, including these sandpipers foraging along the shore.

It was nice to see the Greater and Lesser Yellowlegs together, making their differences, like height and bill size, more apparent.

Western Meadowlark

American Coot

Meandering along the tranquil walking paths here can be a refreshing intermission from a hectic day.

Red Crossbill

Red Crossbill, males & female

Orcas Island, with many natural areas still available for wildlife, is a great place to go birding. Moran State Park is expansive, offering numerous hiking trails.

At our family's cabin overlooking Doe Island, we were thrilled to observe our first Red Crossbill. It was also exciting to witness a House Wren claiming a new birdhouse shortly after Craig's father put it up.

House Wren

Chestnut-backed Chickadee

Purple Finch, male

Orange-crowned Warbler

Small passerines abound here, displaying their attractive colors and songs.

American Goldfinch, male

Pine Siskin

Osprey

Turkey Vulture

Some larger birds often seen soaring near the shore of the island include the fish-catching Osprey and a clean up crew consisting of the Turkey Vulture and Common Raven.

Common Raven

Rough-legged Hawk

Birding in the **Skagit Valley**, especially in the winter, is punctuated with raptors. Access to farm fields, wetland and to Puget Sound makes it particularly appealing to these birds of prey.

Red-tailed Hawk, juvenile

Northern Shrike, juvenile

Northern Harrier, male

Red-tailed Hawk, juvenile

Ring-necked Pheasant, male

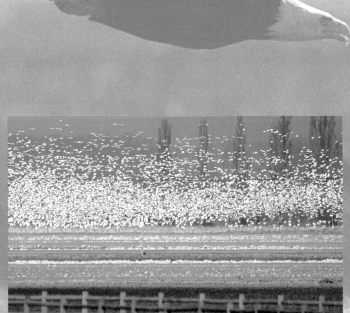
Thousands of Snow Geese on Fir Island

Snow Goose

Gyrfalcon

It was a rare treat to see a Gyrfalcon along the road near Samish Island. We watched it compete for a meal with a Northern Harrier in a nearby field (below). When it returned to a pole after the tussle, one wing was hanging low (left).

Gyrfalcon & Northern Harrier

We spotted this Peregrine Falcon on another telephone pole, which seem to be a favored perch for raptors in the valley.

Red-winged Blackbird, juvenile

Pileated Woodpecker

Common Loon, winter

On the Olympic Peninsula, **Foulweather Bluff** is a protected area owned and maintained by the Nature Conservancy. The varied environment here hosts a treasure trove of bird species. Walking the trail through the woods and out onto the beach, which borders a marsh, there are vantage points to different habitat areas.

Northern Pintail, male

Mew Gulls

Marsh Wren

Great Blue Heron & Trumpeter Swans

Trumpeter Swans, juveniles & adult

Song Sparrow

Closer to urban life, **Everett's waterfront** and **sloughs** are alive with a multitude of waterfowl and other birds. The combination of saltwater from the Sound and fresh-water from the Snohomish River helps to create conditions that are conducive to supporting this avian variety.

Belted Kingfisher, female

Long-billed Curlew, juvenile, July

Least Sandpiper

Caspian Terns & California Gulls

The North end of Everett's Jetty Island offers unique birds, like this visiting Long Billed Curlew, and makes an enjoyable summer day trip.

Green Heron, adult

Green Heron, adult

A small lake and bog area in the city of **Lynnwood**, called Scriber Lake Park, was a perfect place for a pair of Green Heron to be nesting. We were excited to learn of this and visited the area repeatedly in spring and through summer, monitoring the progress of both parents and offspring from a distance.

Green Heron, adult

Nestlings

Nestlings

Nestling

Green Heron, immature

Green Heron, immature

Of the four Green Heron chicks that hatched, at least two survived to make it on their own. It was a delight to watch them hone their hunting skills, snapping at passing dragonflies.

Green Heron, immature

On more than one occasion, birds we were watching at Scriber Lake came closer, as if they were curious about us.

Downy Woodpecker, female

76   Downy Woodpecker, male

Juvenile

Cedar Waxwing pair

This stately Cedar Waxwing displays the brightly colored "wax-dipped" wing tip it is named for.

Cedar Waxwing

Ruby-crowned Kinglet, male

A chorus of songs can be heard from birds around the lake, including the tiny Winter Wren who has the longest song of any bird in North America.

Winter Wren

Bufflehead, male

In addition to the birds perching in trees around it, the park's lake provides a respite for an array of migrating waterfowl each winter.

Mallard, female & chick

Wood Duck, male

Green-winged Teal, male

Hooded Merganser, male & female

Mallard ducklings

White-crowned Sparrow

Bewick's Wren

Chase Lake is a quaint little neighborhood park in South **Edmonds** that some ducks and passerines call home.

We observed this Steller's Jay with wing and tail feathers fanned out over the grass, apparently enjoying the sun on a warm day (a behavior we have witnessed jays performing in our yard). After a short while the jay flew off, going about its business.

Steller's Jay sunbathing in the park

Mallard male & female

Near the waterfront, Edmonds Marsh offers a natural site for birds to live and breed. We spotted our first Virginia Rail here and have seen many other birds, like this Marsh Wren, more regularly from the boardwalk.

Virginia Rail, juvenile

Belted Kingfisher

Glaucous-winged Gull, adult

It is entertaining to watch the antics of the Belted Kingfisher from the Edmonds fishing pier.

Migrating geese and other water-fowl can sometimes be identified from the beach at Brackett's Landing, near the ferry dock.

Brant

Barn Swallow

Purple Martin, male & nestling

Purple Martin, female

Purple Martin, male

Purple Martins utilize man-made nesting cavities during breeding season along **Elliott Bay** in West Seattle.

Great Blue Heron

Gadwall, male

Pied-billed Grebe

Greater White-fronted Goose

The **Montlake Fill**, near the University of Washington campus, is one of Seattle's great areas for urban birding. Gradual restoration of this area to a natural state has encouraged a wide variety of birds to live here or just stop by to rest and forage during migration.

American Coot

Evading a Great Blue Heron that challenged it for its meal, this Osprey flew right overhead with a recent catch along the shore of Lake Washington.

Osprey

Walking the trails throughout
the Fill, one feels far removed
from the bustling city.

Common Yellowthroat, male

Ring-necked Pheasant, male & female

Red-winged Blackbird, male, leucistic

Yellow Warbler, female

Cedar Waxwing

Bullock's Oriole, immature

Juanita Bay Park, on the Eastside of Lake Washington, offers a plethora of birds, which are visible from the walking paths.

(Opposite) Just off the causeway, a group of Red Breasted Sapsuckers busied themselves on a snag.

Violet-green Swallow

American Goldfinch, female

Bushtit, female

Common Yellowthroat, male

Juvenile

Adult

Serendipitous nature moments,
such as being on a quiet beach
near this magnificent Bald Eagle,
are what keep us coming back
for more. Happy birding!

Bald Eagle, adult

Attracting Birds to your yard

Feeders

In the spring and summer, thistle seed (niger seed) is appealing to finch-type birds like this Pine Siskin. A special cylinder feeder with small ports will hold this type of seed.

Hummingbirds require a liquid "nectar" feeder. Keeping their feeder clean with fresh nectar in it is critical, as mold can be toxic to these tiny birds. Avoid mixtures with red dye. These birds are mainly seasonal migrants, but some do winter over and need food all year.

Suet is popular with many types of birds, from woodpeckers to chickadees. There are a variety of mixtures available. We put it out all year, but the birds need it the most during the winter to build up fat reserves when the weather is cold and food is scarce.

Black oil sunflower is the most commonly eaten seed of all. If you had to choose only one food option, this would be it (though offering a variety is preferred). A platform feeder, like this one, or a number of other types of feeders work well to dispense these seeds. It is also available pre-shelled for less mess. We mix ours with a little millet blend as well.

Made from recycled cedar fences

Yard Tips
- Keeping your yard free of pesticides will allow birds a natural supply of insects, an important food source.
- When grooming your yard, leave some long grass blades and other small clippings accessible for nest building materials.
- Planting a variety of native flora is a great way to attract local birds.

Housing
Watching birds move into a house and raise their young can be very rewarding. We have made several successful houses out of boards from old cedar fences. There are also many types of houses to choose from at wild bird supply stores.

Birdbath
A consistent fresh water source is a necessity for wild birds. Observing different birds utilizing a bath in your yard, for drinking or bathing, can bring great pleasure.
- Set the bath up in an area that is protected from potential predators.
- Keep the bath clean and fill it regularly, as the birds will become dependent on a water source.

For more specific information regarding bird feeders or houses, contact your local Audubon Society or consult a wild bird supply store in your area.

Acknowledgements

Special thanks to Frances Wood, author of *Brushed by Feathers: A Year of Birdwatching in the West*, writer of an award-winning newspaper column about birdwatching, and Vice President of the Whidbey Audubon Society. Her assistance and contributions were greatly appreciated.

Our gratitude is also extended to the many people who proofread the book in its various stages before publication.

References

The Birds Of North America Online, Cornell Lab of Ornithology and the American Ornithologists Union. 2004-2005 www.bna.birds.cornell.edu

BirdWeb, Seattle Audubon Society, 2005. www.birdweb.org

Peterson, Roger Tory & Virginia Marie Peterson, *A Field Guide to Western Birds, 3rd ed.*, Boston/NewYork: Houghton Mifflin Company, 1990.

Podulka, Sandy, Ronald W. Rohrbaugh, Jr., and Rick Bonney, Eds., *Handbook of Bird Biology, 2nd Ed.* Ithaca: Princeton University Press, 2004.

Sibley, David Allen, *The Sibley Field Guide to Birds of Western North America*, New York: Alfred A. Knopf, 2003.

Wood Duck, female & duckling

Photographs, graphics & layout by Craig Johnson. Written by Joy Johnson. All photographs were taken with an 80-400mm, f/5.6 lens. Photographs have not been altered other than in page layout.

Bird identification was typically based on a series of photos taken of different angles of the same bird, not just the one photo shown in book.

Wood Duck,

Common Loon, winter

Common Murre, winter

Caspian Tern

Dungeness Spit on the Olympic Peninsula makes a great day hike with miles of sandy beach. We have sighted loons and grebes offshore, along with various gulls and shorebirds closer in. The spit offers an impressive vantage point of the Strait of Juan de Fuca.

Dunlin